# The World According to Jesus

*Twelve Sermons for
Advent, Christmas, and Epiphany*

Michael L. Sherer

CSS Publishing Company, Inc.
Lima, Ohio

THE WORLD ACCORDING TO JESUS
TWELVE SERMONS FOR ADVENT, CHRISTMAS, AND EPIPHANY

FIRST EDITION
Copyright © 2017
by CSS Publishing Co., Inc.

Published by CSS Publishing Company, Inc., Lima, Ohio 45807. All rights reserved. No part of this publication may be reproduced in any manner whatsoever without the prior permission of the publisher, except in the case of brief quotations embodied in critical articles and reviews. Inquiries should be addressed to: CSS Publishing Company, Inc., Permissions Department, 5450 N. Dixie Highway, Lima, Ohio 45807.

---

**Library of Congress Cataloging-in-Publication Data**
Names: Sherer, Michael L., author.
Title: The world according to Jesus : twelve sermons for Advent, Christmas and Epiphany / Michael L. Sherer.
Description: FIRST EDITION. | Lima, Ohio : CSS Publishing Company, Inc., 2017.
Identifiers: LCCN 2017009723| ISBN 9780788029080 (pbk. : alk. paper) | ISBN 0788029088 (pbk. : alk. paper)
Subjects: LCSH: Bible. Gospels--Sermons. | Advent sermons. | Christmas sermons. | Epiphany--Sermons. | Common lectionary (1992). Year B.
Classification: LCC BS2555.54 .S54 2017 | DDC 252/.61--dc23
LC record available at https://lccn.loc.gov/2017009723

---

For more information about CSS Publishing Company resources, visit our website at www.csspub.com, email us at csr@csspub.com, or call (800) 241-4056.

e-book:
ISBN-13: 978-0-7880-2909-7
ISBN-10: 0-7880-2909-6

ISBN-13: 978-0-7880-2908-8
ISBN-10: 0-7880-2908-0      PRINTED IN USA

*For Kathe, Heidi, and Wendy*

# Table of Contents

| | |
|---|---:|
| Advent 1<br>Stay Awake!<br>Mark 13:24-37 | 7 |
| Advent 2<br>Don't Get Stuck!<br>Mark 1:1-8 | 13 |
| Advent 3<br>Get Out of the Jungle!<br>John 1:6-8, 19-28 | 19 |
| Advent 4<br>Jesus Matters<br>Luke 1:26-38 | 23 |
| Christmas Eve / Day<br>Don't Miss This<br>Luke 2:1-14 (15-20) | 29 |
| Christmas 1<br>The Clues Are There<br>Luke 2:22-40 | 35 |
| Baptism of Our Lord<br>To Whom Do You Belong?<br>Mark 1:4-11 | 41 |
| Epiphany 2<br>Bloom Where You Are Planted<br>John 1:43-51 | 47 |

Epiphany 3     51
We Need Some Good News
Mark 1:14-20

Epiphany 4     55
Where's the Authenticity?
Mark 1:21-28

Epiphany 5     59
Be Healed!
Mark 1:29-39

Transfiguration Sunday     63
He's Not Who We Thought
Mark 9:2-9

Advent 1
Mark 13:24-37

## Stay Awake!

*"But in those days, after that suffering, the sun will be darkened, and the moon will not give its light, and the stars will be falling from heaven, and the powers in the heavens will be shaken. Then they will see 'the Son of Man coming in clouds' with great power and glory. Then he will send out the angels, and gather his elect from the four winds, from the ends of the earth to the ends of heaven. "From the fig tree learn its lesson: as soon as its branch becomes tender and puts forth its leaves, you know that summer is near. So also, when you see these things taking place, you know that he is near, at the very gates. Truly I tell you, this generation will not pass away until all these things have taken place. Heaven and earth will pass away, but my words will not pass away. "But about that day or hour no one knows, neither the angels in heaven, nor the Son, but only the Father. Beware, keep alert; for you do not know when the time will come. It is like a man going on a journey, when he leaves home and puts his slaves in charge, each with his work, and commands the doorkeeper to be on the watch. Therefore, keep awake—for you do not know when the master of the house will come, in the evening, or at midnight, or at cockcrow, or at dawn, or else he may find you asleep when he comes suddenly. And what I say to you I say to all: Keep awake."*
Mark 13:24-37

    A young professional woman from Ohio decided to seek her fortune, discern her vocation, and potentially change her life for the better by moving to England. She relocated to London where she began to pursue an advanced degree, seeking new opportunities in the work world.
    One of the things she took with her from the Midwest was an insatiable love for the Chicago Cubs professional

baseball team. She followed the games on the internet, listening to the live feed. The problem with this arrangement was that, when the games began, often around seven or eight o'clock in the evening in the United States, it was one or two o'clock the following morning in London. That made for a very late — or early — bedtime.

In the year when the Cubs were on the cusp of qualifying for the World Series, she eagerly tuned in to listen to the games that would decide who would qualify. But she'd been listening to every Cubs game that year, all broadcast in what was the middle of the night where she lived. After tuning in to the game that was to seal the Cubs' fate, the inevitable happened. She fell asleep and awoke only in time to hear the post-game wrap-up. The Cubs had won. They were in the Series. She had missed all the excitement.

On her Facebook account she lamented, "I've waited years for a moment like this, and of course I slept through it!"

Is there a moral to this story? One might be: Try to get more sleep. Another might be: Try to order your affairs in such a way that you will be alert when events transpire that you believe to be of critical importance to you.

In this young woman's defense, once the World Series began, she stayed awake for every game. Her comment was, "True Cubs fans never give up." And, in demonstration of her commitment to her favorite team, she remained faithful to the last out — staying awake for all of it.

The writer of the gospel of Mark sets the tone for the Christian season of Advent with appropriate advice. "Something important is happening. Stay awake! Don't miss it!"

The context for Mark's good advice is a parable that sounds to many modern readers like an antique story hardly applicable for today. Here's the problem with the parable. As it was originally intended, it undoubtedly presumed that there was to be a cosmic event, an ending of human history of some sort, in the near future for those first readers or hearers of Mark's message.

Mark's gospel reflects this conviction in more than one place. The entire thirteenth chapter of Mark is known to biblical scholars — and most pastors who preach on this gospel — as 'The Little Apocalypse.' An apocalypse was understood to be a rolling up of the scroll of history, a dramatic ending of the current age and the ushering in of a new and different one.

Given the nature of the four New Testament gospels, and the circumstances under which they were written, we have no way of knowing whether Jesus actually said the words — or whether Mark simply created them for his version of Jesus — but we have a remarkable Jesus pronouncement in this gospel. Mark has him promising, or perhaps warning, that there were people alive and listening to him speak who would see the end of the Age. That makes us wonder what Jesus, or at least Mark, thought the end of Age was supposed to look like.

If there truly was to be a cosmic interruption of life on our planet, then Mark's parable, which has Jesus calling his listeners to stay awake, makes perfect sense. But what if the cosmic interruption never came? There's good evidence that, as the first believers imagined it, such an event never occurred. So, then, does the parable say anything to us?

It surely does.

The parable about watching and waiting — and staying awake — has a cosmic meaning the first believers probably never imagined. Here's what it is: At any moment in human history, including our generation, God's surprise interruption of the ordinary flow of things can and does break in. Why should it? Simply put, it's because the universe is grounded in God, who is the source and energy of everything. We don't exist, much less stay alive and thrive and survive, without God's energy flowing into and through us, giving us life and meaning, both now and for the future.

But it is possible to go to sleep on that reality, and suppose life is an accident — or a meaningless joke. You can live your life with no realization whatsoever that the life force that keeps your heart thumping is the life with which God energizes your existence. You can stumble along, wondering where you came from and where you're going.

Or you can wake up.

So, as we launch a brand new church year, what exactly is it that's happening, through which we don't want to be found sleeping? To put it simply, we are in the midst of an invasion, a revolution calculated to upend everything that seems ordinary. Nobody should sleep through a revolution.

The invasion comes from the greatest energy source known to humanity. The living God has created an astonishing universe and brought to life on at least one planet — ours — an incredible ecosystem, ruled (or frequently misruled) by the likes of you and me. And into this unlikely cauldron of human striving and hoping and seeking and doing and stumbling and succeeding, the source of all energy unloads in our midst a generous measure of energizing *dunamis* (a Greek word that gave rise to the English word "dynamite").

Jesus, the Christ, is the agent of God's great gift, the energy that launches a revolution in the human family. In our experience, Jesus the revolutionary comes to us as Spirit power — energy that can turn our lives God-ward. That Spirit power is at work in our midst right now, largely through people who are already caught up in it.

Advent's message is a reminder of something that's also true in March or July — that the Divine Source of all energy is busy, right now, revolutionizing the lives of the people whom God loves. We can be a part of that. Some of us already are. But we can also miss the revolution, simply by sleeping through it.

Stay awake! Stay alive to the power and promises of God. They come at us endlessly, surprisingly, in ways we sometimes least expect. We can miss it. We can sleep through it.

Or we can wake up to the promises — that we are loved, we are God's, and we are people of destiny.

It's Advent. Wake up! And stay awake to the gifts of the power and presence of God in our midst. Those gifts are designed to revolutionize our lives. The revolution goes on. It's going on right now.

Rejoice and be glad!

Advent 2
Mark 1:1-8

# Don't Get Stuck!

*The beginning of the good news of Jesus Christ, the Son of God. As it is written in the prophet Isaiah, "See, I am sending my messenger ahead of you, who will prepare your way; the voice of one crying out in the wilderness: 'Prepare the way of the Lord, make his paths straight,'" John the Baptist appeared in the wilderness, proclaiming a baptism of repentance for the forgiveness of sins. And people from the whole Judean countryside and all the people of Jerusalem were going out to him, and were baptized by him in the river Jordan, confessing their sins. Now John was clothed with camel's hair, with a leather belt around his waist, and he ate locusts and wild honey. He proclaimed, "The one who is more powerful than I is coming after me; I am not worthy to stoop down and untie the thong of his sandals. I have baptized you with water; but he will baptize you with the Holy Spirit."*
Mark 1:1-8

We begin with a modern parable, "a story that never actually happened" but that's still true in some profound way.

Here's the story.

A businessman from a metropolitan area received a registered letter informing him that an entrepreneurial group in another city had decided to honor him with their prestigious "Innovator of the Year" award. He was delighted. On the day of the presentation he allowed himself plenty of time to drive the Interstate, from one community to the other. But at the last minute, his phone rang and he ended up 'putting out a fire,' as they say in the corporate world, handling an unexpected production emergency at his local factory.

Once on the road, running late, he told his GPS device, "Show me a shortcut that will get me to my destination faster than the normal route." Then he turned the task of navigation over to his GPS device, and started out.

To his surprise, somewhere southeast of his city, near the county line, he was instructed to take an exit. He figured it was a trustworthy message, so he turned off. Then he was directed onto a local blacktop. That was fine. But a few miles further on, the blacktop abruptly changed to gravel.

That, he thought, was pretty odd. But he didn't have time to turn around and go back, so he kept going. Then the gravel gave way to dirt. And it had rained the night before, so the dirt was really more like soft mud. He slowed down, but kept going. He began to wonder whether his GPS had lost its mind. He spoke to it. "Are you sure this is the right way?" The metallic-sounding voice replied, "Have I ever let you down before? Just keep going."

Now he was getting nervous, and a little irritated. But he fully expected to see more pavement up ahead at any moment. Instead, the muddy road turned into a pair of tracks, a one-way path that seemed to lead into a field. He thought, *My GPS had better know what it's doing, or it's going to have some explaining to do.* Immediately it struck him as absurd. His GPS had never been known to provide a rationale for anything, much less apologize for a mistake.

Suddenly he saw, up ahead, a barbed wire fence blocking the two-tracks on which he was driving. He coasted up to it and stopped. Through the windshield he found himself staring at a cow, studying him with interest. He climbed out, looked at his tires, and realized he was mired in, up to the hubcaps. He was going to need a tow truck.

Angry, he pulled out his cell phone and called the organizer of the event in the distant city. "I'm going to be late," he admitted, then hung up. Then he speed-dialed AAA and asked for a wrecker. The man on the other end of the line said, "Tell me where you are." He couldn't do it. He tried to describe how he'd gotten there. The tow truck operator said, "I have no idea where you are. Walk to a farmhouse and maybe they can call me and explain it."

He turned off his phone and said to the GPS, "Thanks for nothing." The answer he got was, "We're sorry. This device is experiencing a fatal software flaw. Please navigate by using your wits and your common sense."

Needless to say, he missed the ceremony — and the award.

This story is a parable for our lives. It's drawn from words the writer of Mark attributes to Jesus in today's gospel reading. John the Baptist appeared in the wilderness, proclaiming a "baptism of repentance for the forgiveness of sins."

The Greek word for repentance in this story is *metanoia*. It means, "Change your mind" or "turn around. Stop going the wrong way. Face a healthy direction, and then go there." So, in terms of John the Baptist's words to his listeners, this parable is a cautionary tale about the need to turn around and go a different way.

Could the driver, heading for the award ceremony, have known he was heading for trouble? There were all kinds of signs. Surely when the pavement turned to gravel, he should have known something was amiss. That would have been the time to turn off the GPS and simply follow his better judgment.

How does this apply to us? I'm guessing nobody in this room has been invited to drive to a distant city to accept a prize for innovative creativity (although there's a chance someone in the congregation today actually has). But all of us are on a journey. And our journey through life can best be thought of as a pilgrimage, into God's future. We are here, on this wonderful blue and white planet (as it appears from space) in order to discover what God has in mind for us, and then to do it as best we are able.

What are the signs along the way, that tell us whether we're on the right path, or whether we're heading for disaster? There's a simple answer. We are moving in the right direction when we discern what is good for us, and for the people whom we meet, and with whom we interact, from day to day. If and when it becomes clear that our lives are being enriched, and that theirs are too, because of the choices we make, for ourselves and also on their behalf, then we can be sure that we are on the right path — the one that leads into God's future.

What are the warning signs? Those are pretty clear as well. Every time it becomes obvious that we are doing something, or allowing something to happen, that harms ourselves or another person, we can be certain we've taken a wrong turn. God gave us eyes and ears and our brains in order to read these signs. Sometimes we may not notice, right away, the damage we are doing. But as soon as it becomes clear, then we need to turn, to change direction, to repent.

If someone in your neighborhood — which includes the people you encounter wherever you might find yourself going in the course of a normal day — is experiencing despair of any kind, and you become aware of it but take no action whatsoever to help (or to find someone who could provide the help), then you're on the wrong road. It's time to turn onto a better one. Because, otherwise, both you and that person will surely be diminished, and God's heart will be grieved.

All four of the gospel writers, and also the apostle Paul, talk about repentance — turning, changing direction, getting on a better road. The gospel of Luke does it more consistently and more forcefully than any of the other writers. But Mark was written before Luke, and this first surviving New Testament gospel writer lifts up this important message for the faith community in his very first chapter.

The United Negro College Fund uses a slogan that's useful for all of us. It tells people, "A mind is a terrible thing to waste." That's the message of this gospel story. We can turn our lives away from the path that enriches and fulfills our lives, or we can turn from life's gravel roads and mud tracks onto a road designed just for us — one that refuses to see any human life wasted and thrown away — including our own. Take the better road. Don't get stuck in the mud.

Repentance — changing our mind, turning around — is a good theme on which to meditate during Advent. It's also a good starting point for beginning a new church year. We are accustomed to making 'New Year's resolutions' on the first day of January. There's no need to wait. A great new (church) year's resolution for all of us would be this: I'm ready for something new, something different, a changed direction, a better path. I want to be a child of the light. I want to head down a new road. I know it's why God put me on this planet in the first place.

Happy pilgrimage! And, as you travel that hopeful path, rejoice and be glad!

Advent 3
John 1:6-8, 19-28

# Get Out of the Jungle!

*There was a man sent from God, whose name was John. He came as a witness to testify to the light, so that all might believe through him. He himself was not the light, but he came to testify to the light... This is the testimony given by John when the Jews sent priests and Levites from Jerusalem to ask him, "Who are you?" He confessed and did not deny it, but confessed, "I am not the Messiah." And they asked him, "What then? Are you Elijah?" He said, "I am not." "Are you the prophet?" He answered, "No." Then they said to him, "Who are you? Let us have an answer for those who sent us. What do you say about yourself?" He said, "I am the voice of one crying out in the wilderness, 'Make straight the way of the Lord,'" as the prophet Isaiah said. Now they had been sent from the Pharisees. They asked him, "Why then are you baptizing if you are neither the Messiah, nor Elijah, nor the prophet?" John answered them, "I baptize with water. Among you stands one whom you do not know, the one who is coming after me; I am not worthy to untie the thong of his sandal." This took place in Bethany across the Jordan where John was baptizing.*
John 1:6-8, 19-28

Once upon a time there lived a pair of twins, a boy and a girl, whose parents decided to teach them survival skills. What they were told was, "It's a jungle out there. You have to be ready for it. You need to be tough. You need to learn to defend yourselves — or your enemies will devour you."

And so, the twins grew up learning to follow their parents' often-repeated advice: "Trust no one; suspect everyone." One consequence of this training was that the twins were always on the defensive. They tended to be argumentative with those who tried to befriend them. They became judgmental in the extreme, since neither of them could ever be sure that others were people of good will. And they tended to become xenophobic — highly suspicious of people who were not like them. Not surprisingly, they saw the same attitudes, patterns, and behaviors in their parents.

Once the two youngsters graduated from high school and left home, they took different paths. The young woman continued to nurture an adversarial relationship with nearly everyone she met. She developed a few close friends, but they were all of the same mind as was she. When they got together socially, it was like being in an echo chamber. They were all of the same mind, and their times together only reinforced their shared opinions.

The young man ended up in a work environment with so much diversity that he soon had to confront his own world view. Few of his colleagues shared it. In time, he began to think differently. He realized that some of those who became his best friends had points of view completely different from his. And yet, they liked him, respected his opinions, and even taught him to laugh at himself once in a while.

Then the inevitable happened. The twins came home for Thanksgiving dinner at their parents' home. Quickly it became obvious it was going to be three-against-one. Parents and daughter took on their son and his "errant, revisionist ideas" and savaged him mercilessly. There was ridicule, scorn, sarcasm — the full package. The young man considered ditching his family and walking out before the meal was even served. But he thought of his new friends at work, and then he did something remarkable.

To his family he said, "You know what? I've encountered some very wise people in my journey through life so far. And one of them pointed out that when people talk like and behave you do — like I used to do — they're really prisoners of their primitive brain, the reptilian part that knows how to fight or run from people who are their enemies. But living like that is a dead end. It's like living in a jungle. There's nothing fulfilling about it. You're never going to grow and learn and make the world a better place."

His parents and sister stared at him in disbelief. He said, "You don't have to agree with me, and you don't have to serve me Thanksgiving dinner if you don't want to. But this is who I am now. And I don't want to live in the jungle anymore."

What does this imaginary tale have to do with the season of Advent? Just this: It is our nature, as human beings, to want to deceive ourselves into believing that the world is a jungle, and that people who are not like us are out to get us. Even those of us within Christian congregations find ourselves slipping into this pattern at times. Other people don't have the truth, but we do. Other people don't know how to worship properly, but we do. Other people don't think or look or even smell like we do, so they probably "wouldn't be comfortable" in our congregation.

It is our nature to gravitate toward "jungle thinking." It can cripple our lives and impoverish our souls. To give in to such "primitive brain behavior" is to descend into a very dark place.

Into such a world comes John the Baptist, announcing the coming into our darkness of One who is and who brings transforming, life-giving light. John was not the Light, but came to bear witness to the Light, we are told in the Fourth gospel. What does that mean?

Jesus comes to us with a better way. Instead of us cowering in the darkness, he calls us to embrace the light. Instead of judging others out of hand, he calls us to open ourselves to them, and to take the chance that we might discover the humanity within them. Instead of hating what is unfamiliar and seemingly threatening, he calls us to learn to celebrate the diversity in our world, because God is a God of diversity and obviously loves it enough to have created and embraced it.

Jesus comes to us with an invitation. Let us step out of our cave, our smug self-righteousness, our dark night of false security, and embrace the life God has prepared for us. John the gospel writer summarizes where the Light leads and what it promises to create. Jesus, as the gospel writer describes him, declares, "I have come that you may have life — in all its abundance" (John 10:10).

It needs to be recognized that viewing other people with openness, trust, and compassion — rather than with suspicion and fear — is counterintuitive. There's nothing normal about it. Nobody would automatically choose to view the world that way. The reason is clear. Our primitive brain is powerful. It tends to override our more benevolent instincts. Given that reality, there is no good reason to believe that what William Shakespeare so poetically called 'the better angels of our nature' will ever take charge. And that explains why we need an intervention.

That intervention has already happened, and it continues to happen. Our dark path gets interrupted in the most unexpected way. There is no logical reason in the world that we human beings should be given a surprise alternative to our own worst instincts. But that's what we have. Our natural inclination is to swim in a dark swamp. But now we have an option. There's a path into a bright future. There's a jungle out there — and there's also a light-filled, hopeful, healthy alternative.

Let us get out of the jungle! Let us embrace the light, because the light is ready and eager to embrace us. When that happens, there will be a transformation — and our lives will never be the same again.

Rejoice and be glad!

Advent 4
Luke 1:26-38

# Jesus Matters

*In the sixth month the angel Gabriel was sent by God to a town in Galilee called Nazareth, to a virgin engaged to a man whose name was Joseph, of the house of David. The virgin's name was Mary. And he came to her and said, "Greetings, favored one! The Lord is with you." But she was much perplexed by his words and pondered what sort of greeting this might be. The angel said to her, "Do not be afraid, Mary, for you have found favor with God. And now, you will conceive in your womb and bear a son, and you will name him Jesus. He will be great, and will be called the Son of the Most High, and the Lord God will give to him the throne of his ancestor David. He will reign over the house of Jacob forever, and of his kingdom there will be no end." Mary said to the angel, "How can this be, since I am a virgin?" The angel said to her, "The Holy Spirit will come upon you, and the power of the Most High will overshadow you; therefore the child to be born will be holy; he will be called Son of God. And now, your relative Elizabeth in her old age has also conceived a son; and this is the sixth month for her who was said to be barren. For nothing will be impossible with God." Then Mary said, "Here am I, the servant of the Lord; let it be with me according to your word." Then the angel departed from her.*
Luke 1:26-38

    It is difficult for people in the faith community, 2,000 years after the Christian movement began, to imagine — much less appreciate — what it was like to stand up for Jesus. To put it mildly, it was incredibly difficult.
    The first believers knew something extraordinary. Their hero, who had been murdered by a foreign power occupying

their country, was somehow alive and back with them, encountering and encouraging them in the midst of their lives. There was no explaining how a dead hero could be alive once again — although lots of early Christians tried their hand at it — but, in their experience, there was also no denying it.

As the story went out that the rabbi from Nazareth was not dead and wasn't going away, the pushback was predictable. It came from the most logical place — the community out of which the Jesus movement grew. Leaders of the first-century Jewish faith community recognized a serious threat when they saw one. Followers of The Way, as they came to be called, were beginning to coax members away from Judaism and into Jewish Christianity.

If you had been a leader in an ancient and well-established religious movement when some of your own former faith colleagues were beginning to pull away, and to take more and more of your community with them, and seem to be becoming a growing threat to you, what would you do? The Jewish faith community did the most logical thing they could think of. They decided to kill the brand new Jesus movement in its cradle, before it could grow and do real damage. How did they do it? They developed a simple strategy.

The argument went out from the enemies of the Jesus movement that Jesus wasn't important — because Jesus didn't matter. The argument went like this: We have had a lot of charismatic teachers and preachers in Israel. Jesus is no different. None of them claimed they would come back from the dead. Jesus didn't either. That, his enemies said, was a fiction created by his followers. They have, it was suggested, invented this 'Jesus-is-alive' myth. But it's just that — a fiction. And Jesus is a fly-by-night self-proclaimed charismatic leader. He lived. He died. He's gone. He doesn't matter.

This was the challenge the first Christians faced. Their enemies were trying to get rid of Christianity by getting rid of Jesus. And members of Jesus' faith community, who were convinced beyond the shadow of a doubt that he was alive and with them — and leading them into the future — began to look for ways to show that Jesus really does matter. And they wanted to take the starch out of their Jewish neighbors' arguments when they did it.

We see signs of this in the first chapter of the gospel of Luke. This Jesus champion, like the other gospel writers, is looking for ways of convincing whoever will pay attention that Jesus does indeed matter. Nowadays we are inclined to say that the arguments Luke used are not particularly convincing, but they may have been at the time.

At the beginning of his gospel, Luke uses two arguments designed to convince his readers — or listeners — that Jesus truly does matter. The first argument is this: Luke tells us that Jesus is descended from David, the great king. It was an argument aimed directly at the Jewish church. It's hard to tell whether this claim was designed more to convince Christians or Jews. It may have been Luke's way of saying, "Our claim to King David is better than your claim to King David — and Jesus is his direct descendant."

It probably didn't convince Jews, but it may have impressed the first Christians.

The second argument Luke makes is this: Jesus' father was God the Almighty, not some human being. This sounds sensational to us, but it may not have for the first Christians. The same claim was made for many great men in antiquity. Emperor Augustus Caesar was believed to have had a divine father. So was Alexander the Great. Often these stories arose after a famous man had died.

In Jesus' case, we call this idea "The Virgin Birth." It seems puzzling that Luke makes this claim for Jesus, for two reasons. First, it made Jesus sound like any other famous man in the history of Greece and Rome. Second, it contradicts the argument, also made by Luke, that Jesus is a direct descendant of King David. The problem comes when we read the genealogy for Jesus that Luke includes in his gospel. That genealogy concludes that Jesus was a descendant from David through Joseph, not Mary. And so, if the Virgin Birth is true, then the descendancy from David cannot be true. The opposite is also the case.

Why did Luke include two contradictory claims for Jesus in his gospel? The best answer we can imagine is that this writer wants to make the argument, any way he can, that Jesus truly does matter. Perhaps Luke believed that, if one argument didn't convince his readers, the other would. It's pretty clear that the Jewish enemies of the faith community weren't convinced by either argument.

Why does any of this matter for us on this fourth and final Sunday in the Advent season? Here's why. Christians have always been certain that, when all is said and done, Jesus truly does matter for the faith community. All sorts of arguments have been used to try to prove this to be true. None of the arguments are persuasive in and of themselves. But there's a reason the faith community has tried so hard to say and show that Jesus really does matter.

The reason is: it's true. Jesus matters more than we can say.

How does he matter — and why?

Jesus matters because his life and his death and his abiding presence in our lives show us what God means for our lives. Without Jesus' life among us, we would be left wondering. So, given the life and death and abiding presence of Jesus, what does God mean for us?

Jesus shows us that God means for us to know that we are loved with an impossibly generous love. There is nothing we can do to deserve it, nor to pay for it. The one and only authentic response to that generosity is to love others — including our enemies. Such a response will transform our lives and begin to redeem the world. This is an astonishing Christmas gift to us, by the way.

That's who Jesus was and is. And that's why — and how — Jesus matters.

As we come now to the celebration of Jesus' birth, let us remember why the day and celebration matter. They matter for us because Jesus matters, and always has, and always will.

Rejoice and be glad!

Christmas Eve / Day
Luke 2:1-14 (15-20)

# Don't Miss This

*In those days a decree went out from Emperor Augustus that all the world should be registered. This was the first registration and was taken while Quirinius was governor of Syria. All went to their own towns to be registered. Joseph also went from the town of Nazareth in Galilee to Judea, to the city of David called Bethlehem, because he was descended from the house and family of David. He went to be registered with Mary, to whom he was engaged and who was expecting a child. While they were there, the time came for her to deliver her child. And she gave birth to her firstborn son and wrapped him in bands of cloth, and laid him in a manger, because there was no place for them in the inn. In that region there were shepherds living in the fields, keeping watch over their flock by night. Then an angel of the Lord stood before them, and the glory of the Lord shone around them, and they were terrified. But the angel said to them, "Do not be afraid; for see—I am bringing you good news of great joy for all the people: to you is born this day in the city of David a Savior, who is the Messiah, the Lord. This will be a sign for you: you will find a child wrapped in bands of cloth and lying in a manger." And suddenly there was with the angel a multitude of the heavenly host, praising God and saying, "Glory to God in the highest heaven, and on earth peace among those whom he favors!" When the angels had left them and gone into heaven, the shepherds said to one another, "Let us go now to Bethlehem and see this thing that has taken place, which the Lord has made known to us." So they went with haste and found Mary and Joseph, and the child lying in the manger. When they saw this, they made known what had been told them about this child; and all who heard it were amazed at what the shepherds told them. But Mary treasured all these words and pondered them*

*in her heart. The shepherds returned, glorifying and praising God for all they had heard and seen, as it had been told them.*
Luke 2:1-14 (15-20)

Pastors are often warned, before they leave the seminary, not to say certain things in the pulpit. One of those things is this: "Never say to your congregation, 'Of course we all know the Bible story of [fill in the blank].' "

Why shouldn't a pastor say that during a sermon? The reason is that, in our day fewer and fewer people actually know what's in the Bible. They don't recognize the stories. The preacher needs to tell the story first, as if it's a brand new one.

Pastors are taught something else in seminary as well. It is this: "On certain occasions, including Christmas Eve and Easter morning, you will have large congregations full of visitors, many of whom will not have been at worship for months, if at all. Don't waste the opportunity to share something with them that could possibly change their lives for the better."

Both of the things I just mentioned come into play tonight. As to the second thing pastors are to be careful about, some of us at worship right now have not been here for a while. Perhaps some of us are at worship for the first time. So this would not be a good time to waste a message that could be life-changing for some of you.

As to the first thing pastors are asked to avoid, for once we're faced with an exception to the rule. As it turns out, this may be one of the few times when it is safe to assume that everyone in this room actually knows the Bible story on which tonight's message is based. The story of shepherds in a field outside Bethlehem, encountering angels and hurrying into town to find a stable and a manger and a brand new baby, may be the most familiar Bible story of all time.

Why is that? It's because it's the story line for annual Christmas pageants, staged by children for their parents, grandparents, aunts, uncles, and other friends of the family. Some of you in the congregation tonight may actually have worn a bathrobe, pretending to be a shepherd, once or twice in your youth.

So, in violation of the rule set by countless seminary professors, it's probably safe to say it to you tonight: "We all know this story very well. We know it so well, we are in danger of missing the real message."

What is the real message in the story of the shepherds, watching over their flocks in the fields out beyond Bethlehem? There is no clear agreement about it. Here, however, is one of the themes that it seems certain Luke, the writer of this story, wants us to hear.

The story of Jesus' birth and ministry and murder and reappearance to his followers represents an extraordinary series of events. The meaning of Jesus is the meaning of God for our lives. And whoever wrote the gospel of Luke is worried about something. He's concerned that people will become aware of Jesus but miss what he means. People may even have an encounter with Jesus and not understand why Jesus matters.

The shepherds in this story got the message. Something extraordinary was beginning with the birth of Jesus, and Luke tells us that the shepherds got the message. You might be tempted to say, "Well, sure, but they had an advantage. There were angels helping them figure it out." That may not be a very convincing argument. If you or I were poverty-stricken and uneducated, low-life and dirty, as shepherds typically were in first-century Palestine, the appearance of angels overhead might have caused one of at least two results.

These fellows may have concluded they were hallucinating. That would not have led them to go into town. It might have convinced them to run for cover.

Or, the shepherds may have concluded the angels were the real deal, leading them to the same conclusion — that the smart thing to do would be to run for their lives. Evidently Luke inserted the detail that the angels told the shepherds not to be afraid, for exactly that reason.

In other words, seeing angels overhead would not have made it any easier for the shepherds to believe there was something extraordinary going on. But that's not Luke's point. The writer wants to say that some unexceptional people — the shepherds — got the message, and didn't miss out on the importance of who Jesus is — even while hardly anybody else did.

Where were the townspeople in Bethlehem, according to this story? Luke would tell us that they wouldn't have been interested. Where was the mayor? Where was the welcoming committee? Well, actually, that's who the shepherds became.

What is the real point of this story? Why do you need shepherds in this story in the first place? Here's why: The shepherds are symbolic of people who don't matter very much. Keep in mind that Luke wrote his story of Jesus after he knew the ending. Jesus had been betrayed, murdered, and returned to the presence of his followers. From that perspective, Luke backs up and tells the beginning of the story.

Hardly any credible Bible scholar believes that anybody, including Luke, really knew anything factual about Jesus' birth. Only Luke and Matthew try to imagine what really happened, and they don't agree. Matthew says Jesus' home town was Bethlehem. Luke says it was Nazareth.

So we're not dealing with history here. This is a story about who Jesus is and what Jesus means for people — including people like us. Luke knows what kind of people first decided to follow Jesus. He knew what they were like because he had met a lot of them. And, before long, those first believers wanted to know about Jesus' birth. It may seem troubling to us, but what Luke seems to have done was to give people what they were asking for. He may have decided, "We don't have a story about Jesus' birth, so I'll write one."

And when he did it, Luke decided that the people who ended up taking Jesus' birth seriously would have been the ones who took the adult Jesus seriously. They were not the ones you'd put on a list of the movers and shakers, the ones with influence. Luke gives us shepherds — outsiders, poor people, the disenfranchised, people who probably could use a bath but don't have access to a nice warm shower.

The ordinary people who responded to Jesus knew one thing for certain. Jesus matters. The meaning of his life is the meaning of God for our own lives. It's a life that changes lives, when people catch on to what he said and did and promised — not only for marginalized people, but for anybody who will pay attention. The shepherds paid attention. Something extraordinary began when Jesus arrived in our midst. Everybody could have missed it. Many people did. But some didn't. Ordinary people caught on. Servants did. Slaves did. Women, who had no rights in the first century, frequently did.

That's who the shepherds represent. And as the gospel of Luke unfolds, there are many others just like them — people with no options, no rights, no money, very little food, hardly any hope. When they encountered Jesus, it changed their lives.

Tonight we have an opportunity to encounter Jesus — the adult Jesus, the no-longer-in-the-manger Jesus, the life-changing Jesus.

In our imagination right now, on this special, rather enchanting night, Jesus is lying in a manger. But that isn't where he stays. He grows up. He shows us how our lives can change, entirely for the better. He brings a message of promise and hope.

Rejoice and be glad!

Christmas 1
Luke 2:22-40

# The Clues Are There

*When the time came for their purification according to the law of Moses, they brought him up to Jerusalem to present him to the Lord (as it is written in the law of the Lord, "Every firstborn male shall be designated as holy to the Lord"), and they offered a sacrifice according to what is stated in the law of the Lord, "a pair of turtledoves or two young pigeons." Now there was a man in Jerusalem whose name was Simeon; this man was righteous and devout, looking forward to the consolation of Israel, and the Holy Spirit rested on him. It had been revealed to him by the Holy Spirit that he would not see death before he had seen the Lord's Messiah. Guided by the Spirit, Simeon came into the temple; and when the parents brought in the child Jesus, to do for him what was customary under the law, Simeon took him in his arms and praised God, saying, "Master, now you are dismissing your servant in peace, according to your word; for my eyes have seen your salvation, which you have prepared in the presence of all peoples, a light for revelation to the Gentiles and for glory to your people Israel." And the child's father and mother were amazed at what was being said about him. Then Simeon blessed them and said to his mother Mary, "This child is destined for the falling and the rising of many in Israel, and to be a sign that will be opposed so that the inner thoughts of many will be revealed — and a sword will pierce your own soul too." There was also a prophet, Anna the daughter of Phanuel, of the tribe of Asher. She was of a great age, having lived with her husband seven years after her marriage, then as a widow to the age of eighty-four. She never left the temple but worshiped there with fasting and prayer night and day. At that moment she came, and began to praise God and to speak about the child to all who were looking for the redemption of Jerusalem. When they had finished everything required by the law of the Lord, they re-*

*turned to Galilee, to their own town of Nazareth. The child grew and became strong, filled with wisdom; and the favor of God was upon him.*
Luke 2:22-40

Three of the programs embedded in the popular "Masterpiece Mystery" television series on Public Television are set in the university town of Oxford, England. Each episode, in any and all of the three series, begins in the same way. A string of seemingly unrelated incidents follow, one after another, in rapid succession. The viewer is left to wonder whether what's been presented is not simply window dressing before the 'real' story begins.

A typical episode might begin something like this. We see a young man riding a bicycle when he is nearly sideswiped on a narrow street. Then we are on the university campus, where a harried professor is dashing from one location to the next. Then we see a woman working in her garden. Then comes a street scene somewhere in the city. Then there is a nightclub, where a youngster is dancing beneath strobe lights. Then comes the organ loft in a local church, where a musician is playing a piece by J.S. Bach.

The list of shapshots goes on and on, until the viewer is nearly dizzy with them.

Those who watch these programs with regularity know that none of the opening incidents are incidental. One dare not ignore any of them. All of them will be important for the story that is about to unfold. Often, if the program is re-run at a later date, the viewer who watches it for the second time realizes the significance of some or all of these opening sequences in ways that was not initially appreciated.

What has any of this got to do with an old man and a baby and the Great Temple in Jerusalem in BCE 4? Just this.

The writer of Luke's gospel story has embedded clues in his narrative. They are not immediately apparent to the reader or the hearer. One may ask why some of these details even need to be in the story — or whether they are throwaway ornaments, simply inserted in order to make the tale sound more interesting.

Be not deceived. Luke knows what he's doing. Everything is there for a reason.

Luke is the only gospel writer who gives us a story about two elderly seekers who frequent the national shrine of the Jewish church. That in itself is a clue. Luke cares about vulnerable people. No one is more vulnerable than an aging man and an equally aged woman, nearing life's end.

One could view Simeon and Anna as has-beens, people whose years have nearly run out and who don't matter anymore. Luke presents them to us as individuals who have something to contribute, even in — or perhaps, especially because of — old age. (This concern for the vulnerable elderly surfaces again in Luke's second book of scripture, the Acts of the Apostles, where the first faith community, in Jerusalem, devises a system to care for aging widows.)

But the story of Simeon and Anna contains another clue to this gospel writer's priorities. Luke wants to introduce to his readers and hearers, including us, a theme that will return several more times in his story. Arguably, we already heard this theme in Luke's version of the story of Jesus' birth. Only in Luke do we have a story about shepherds — marginalized, unimportant, unkempt castoffs from "respectable society" — being elevated to a place of great importance.

The theme sounded in today's text mirrors this 'lifting up' of lowly people. It comes in a sentence spoken by Simeon, one that many readers of this story are inclined to dismiss as unimportant — or perhaps no more than the rambling thoughts of a senile old codger. Be not deceived. When Luke adds a detail to his story, he puts it there for a reason. What Simeon has to say is not unimportant.

Here's what Simeon says about Jesus, who is still an infant. "This child is destined for the falling and rising of many in Israel, and to be a sign that will be opposed so that the inner thoughts of many will be revealed."

Does that really make any sense? Is it supposed to?

In terms of the way Luke tells the rest of his story, we might say it makes about as much sense as an incident in an English mystery story in which a young man is almost sideswiped on his bicycle, heading up a narrow alley, toward a driver coming down the other direction. (Spoiler information: in that particular episode, the driver was trying to kill the cyclist in order to cover up his own culpability in a crime about which the biker had some crucial information. We learn that later.)

Simeon's cryptic words to Jesus' parents amount to what some teachers of literature would call foreshadowing. Luke will raise this theme again, many times, in his gospel. At this point, early in the story, the reader or hearer is getting a heads up. (It foreshadows what is to come later.)

When a story-teller uses foreshadowing, he or she is saying to us, who read or hear the story, "Don't be surprised about what's coming. I've given you clues. You've been warned."

What is the meaning of 'the falling and rising of many' about which Simeon speaks? Luke spells it out later on, most dramatically in a parable about an obscenely wealthy man who lives in a walled mansion. In the street outside his gate lies a starving beggar. Will the overfed rich man make a move to help feed the beggar? Not on your life. Luke uses the parable to illustrate what for him is a key truth about social standing. Theologians call it the principle of 'reversal.'

The tables are turned and everything is reversed in the parable of the rich man and the starving beggar. The rich man goes to hell and can't even get a drink of water to cool his tongue. The beggar goes to heaven and can't begin to eat all the food that's set before him.

The rich becomes poor. The poor becomes rich. Reversal!

Jesus went about, according to Luke, teaching and preaching reversal. To poor, hungry, marginalized people (like the Bethlehem shepherds, by the way) reversal was sensationally good news. "We won't always be poor. The rich won't always be lording it over us."

Since we know that is a key theme in Luke, we can now make sense of Simeon's words in the Jerusalem Temple, to Jesus' parents: "This child is destined for the falling and the rising of many in Israel, and to be a sign that will be opposed."

Translation: Jesus' mission is to preach and promise reversal. And when he does that, there will be significant pushback. The final result will be crucifixion, something that Simeon promises (threatens?) will pierce his mother's soul.

According to Luke, that's what happened to Mary.

What does Luke's story about Simeon and his cryptic promise have to do with us? It comes as both warning and promise — law and gospel.

If we ally ourselves with the privileged of this world, at the expense of our suffering brothers and sisters, there will be a price.

But if we declare and show solidarity with the vulnerable of our planet, speaking truth to power where and when the wealthy victimize the helpless, there will be a reward. The reward is not necessarily that we'll get to go to heaven and gorge ourselves on too much food. (That may or may not happen; we'll leave that to God.) Instead, the promise for us is, simply, that we will have a role in ushering in God's peace and healing, and will have the satisfaction of knowing that we were and are way-clearers for the in-breaking of the reign of the Creator in our midst.

The reign of God is not somewhere out there, in the distant future. It is here. It has begun. And we can be a part of it, right now.

Rejoice and be glad!

Baptism of Our Lord
Mark 1:4-11

# To Whom Do You Belong?

*John the Baptist appeared in the wilderness, proclaiming a baptism of repentance for the forgiveness of sins. And people from the whole Judean countryside and all the people of Jerusalem were going out to him, and were baptized by him in the river Jordan, confessing their sins. Now John was clothed with camel's hair, with a leather belt around his waist, and he ate locusts and wild honey. He proclaimed, "The one who is more powerful than I is coming after me; I am not worthy to stoop down and untie the thong of his sandals. I have baptized you with water; but he will baptize you with the Holy Spirit." In those days Jesus came from Nazareth of Galilee and was baptized by John in the Jordan. And just as he was coming up out of the water, he saw the heavens torn apart and the Spirit descending like a dove on him. And a voice came from heaven, "You are my Son, the Beloved; with you I am well pleased."*
Mark 1:4-11

We begin with a story, some of which actually happened, and some of which did not. It will be left to the listener to try to imagine which parts are which.

A young schoolboy was accustomed to having his father come to fetch him at the end of each class day and bring him home. Since he was only a first-grader and the school was located in a large metropolitan area, there was no way his parents would allow him to walk home by himself. Because his home was not within the zone where the school buses ran, he understood he should wait for his father to come.

And so he did — faithfully, day after day. But on one occasion, because his father was busy doing errands connected to his profession, he simply forgot the time and did not come to pick up the youngster. And so the boy sat on the front steps of the school building and waited. Three o'clock gave way to three-thirty and then to four. Finally, at four-thirty, the last staff person to leave the school building came out onto the front steps, where she encountered the little boy.

Sitting down next to him, she asked solicitously, "Do you go to school here?"

Came the transparent answer, "Yes. I go here every day."

The school employee said, "Whose little boy are you? Who do you belong to? And why are you sitting here all alone?"

The child cheerfully responded, "My daddy is coming to pick me up."

"Is he late?" Came the next query.

"I don't know," the youngster replied. "I don't know what time it is."

Just then a car pulled up at the curb. The child's father leaped from the driver's seat and hurried to the front steps. "I am so sorry," he exclaimed, scooping the young student up into his arms. "I completely forgot to come to get you today."

The staff person looked uncertainly at the boy, whose expression made it clear this was indeed his parent. Then she looked at his father, flashed a glance of disapproval, and quickly took her leave.

The boy's father said, "Didn't you worry when I didn't come right away?"

"Oh no," the youngster replied. "You said you would come. I knew you would. And now, here you are."

His father felt a lump in his throat and tears welling in his eyes. He carried his son to the car and deposited him safely on the passenger seat for the journey home.

As they rode along, the child turned to his father and said, "That nice lady asked me, 'Who do you belong to?' Didn't she know I belong to you?"

As suggested at the outset, some of this story is true. It's a cautionary tale and, in some ways, a scary one. But it illustrates one clear truth. When we know to whom we belong, and we trust implicitly that it is indeed true, it makes all the difference in the world.

The story about Jesus' baptism is about several things. Underlying the story, in this case told by the writer of the earliest gospel, Mark, is the theme of belonging. At the outset of his ministry, Jesus needed to know what we need to know: To whom do you belong?

Why does it matter?

When we know whose we are, we are able to discern who we are. This is the meaning of Christian baptism. This practice is at least as old as the Jordan River ministry of John the Baptist. Over the centuries it has had a sometimes tortured history. Christians have fought over the method of its administration and whether or not it should be considered a sacrament of the church. Some believers have even found ways to celebrate it without actually using water.

One thing is constant, however. To be baptized in the Christian community means to open one's self to the claim and the promise of a gracious God. It is to say, "I know to whom I belong. I want that claim on me to shape who I am and who I become." If and when we baptize an infant, we are saying the same thing, on behalf of the small child. We are saying, "I (or we) want for this child the benefits and the promise that God has already made for him or her."

And so we pour the water — or we immerse the candidate — in this sacred rite of initiation.

Anyone who reads or hears the story of Jesus' baptism cannot help but ask a question about why he submitted to this practice. By the end of the first century, when the gospel of John, the last one written, had begun to circulate, there was among believers the suspicion or the outright belief that Jesus was in fact divine. And, if that were the case, why did baptism make sense in his case?

There is more than one way to address this concern. Matthew, Luke, and John all suggest there was divinity in the person of Jesus at least from his birth. In Matthew's case, the writer has Jesus declare that his baptism was necessary "to fulfill all righteousness." Luke offers no explanation at all. And in John's case, there is simply no story about Jesus' baptism.

Some theologians have suggested that, in the case of both Matthew and Luke, the divinity of Jesus does not enter the equation at all, since neither of these writers may actually have believed that Jesus was divine. This sounds shocking to some believers, until they consider that both Matthew and Luke include both a virgin birth story and a genealogy for Jesus. The virgin birth idea requires belief that Jesus didn't have an earthly father. But the genealogies in both these gospels require the reader to understand that Joseph was Jesus' biological parent.

Did Matthew and Luke believe Jesus was divine from birth? It's hard to know. Both of them appear to be of two minds about it. If the answer is that they are either unsure or ambivalent, which appears to be the case, then Jesus' baptism is not problematic in the least.

But the text for today is not from Matthew, Luke, or John. It is Mark's story. And Mark declares that Jesus was declared to be God's special person at the moment of his baptism. It is Mark's way of telling his readers and hearers, "Now you know who Jesus is — and whose he is."

It is the same with us. When we were baptized — or, when we will be if this is a coming event for any of us — we are declaring or having declared for us, "Now we know, for certain and for all time, who we are and whose we are." Once we are sure about that, we can live and love and serve and celebrate and die safe in the arms of a loving God.

That first-grader, sitting on the front steps of the school building, waited without doubt or fear for the arrival of one who cared for him and who would not abandon him. He was able to do that because he knew who he was; and he knew that because he knew with utter certainty whose he was.

As believers loved and embraced by a gracious God, we can know that too.

Rejoice and be glad!

Epiphany 2
John 1:43-51

# Bloom Where You Are Planted

*The next day Jesus decided to go to Galilee. He found Philip and said to him, "Follow me." Now Philip was from Bethsaida, the city of Andrew and Peter. Philip found Nathanael and said to him, "We have found him about whom Moses in the law and also the prophets wrote, Jesus son of Joseph from Nazareth." Nathanael said to him, "Can anything good come out of Nazareth?" Philip said to him, "Come and see." When Jesus saw Nathanael coming toward him, he said of him, "Here is truly an Israelite in whom there is no deceit!" Nathanael asked him, "Where did you get to know me?" Jesus answered, "I saw you under the fig tree before Philip called you." Nathanael replied, "Rabbi, you are the Son of God! You are the King of Israel!" Jesus answered, "Do you believe because I told you that I saw you under the fig tree? You will see greater things than these." And he said to him, "Very truly, I tell you, you will see heaven opened and the angels of God ascending and descending upon the Son of Man."*
John 1:43-51

    Wilhelm Loehe was a young pastor in Bavaria, the southeastern corner of Germany. He finished his theological studies in the early 1840s and began to think about where he might like to serve as a parish pastor.

    Loehe had some characteristics that were viewed by some as virtues, by others as liabilities. He was idealistic, determined, courageous, outspoken, and — in the minds of his detractors — brash. While studying theology, he had come to the conclusion that his expression of Christianity, the Evangelical Lutheran Church in Bavaria, was too worldly. It was giving in to relativizing what he believed was a clear and pure gospel message, one not to be compromised.

Loehe was especially concerned about the confessional stance of the church in his generation. He wanted a clear, solid, straightforward approach to Christian doctrine to be lifted up. This did not sit well with the more accommodating leadership of the church in Bavaria. Even though he was a gifted preacher, one who appeared to have a great future awaiting him in what could have been one of the large, prestigious congregations in the city of Nuremberg, his superiors saw to it that he got no reward for what they saw to be his stubborn impertinence.

And so, when it came time for Loehe to be assigned to a congregation, he got the shock of his life. Instead of being added to the ministerial staff of a large city parish, he was assigned to a backwater — a village with an almost unspellable and unpronounceable name, one that many considered to be 'a mudhole of a place.'

In the village of Neuendettelsau [a pronouncer for proclaimers: Noy-en-DETT-el-sow], the young clergyman could have fallen into despair and cursed his very bad luck. But he didn't. He decided to put his considerable gifts for ministry to work and, to borrow a phrase, to "bloom where he was planted."

Another phrase was probably in the back of his mind. It would have been a line from today's gospel reading. "Can any good thing come out of [a dead-end village] Nazareth?" Can any good thing come out of a mud hole like Neuendettelsau?

Loehe spent his entire ministry there. Over time, the Lutheran congregation at Neuendettelsau, once considered to be on its last legs and ready to be shut down, became a thriving and rapidly growing faith community. Loehe was responsible for turning his 'mudhole of a place' into a thriving ministry center. His parish gave birth to schools for children and adults, training centers for deaconesses and missionary pastors, a hospital, and an orphanage.

One-hundred-fifty years later, tourists visiting in Saint Lorenz, the largest Lutheran congregation in Nuremberg, Germany, are greeted with displays describing the significant ministry and mission outreach work of the Bavarian Lutheran Church. An interesting, and highly ironic, sentence in that display declares, "If you want to see this ministry being carried out at its best, you need to visit the village of Neuendettelsau."

Can any good thing come out of a mud-hole? Can any good thing come out of a dying inner-city congregation? Out of a tiny group in a suburban church trying to do something to improve the world in some small way? Out of a handful of committed church folk eager to change their neighborhood, their block, their town or city, when the group is only populated by pious nobodies?

The implied answer in today's gospel is a resounding Yes! In fact, that's where good things have almost always come from.

I doubt Jesus' friends and relatives ever told him to "bloom where you're planted." That expression belongs to our age, not theirs. In fact, there's every chance that the people who knew Jesus as a youth and a young adult may have entertained serious doubts about him ever amounting to anything much. Like Loehe, they may have found him to be pushy, overly-idealistic, rash, and totally unrealistic.

We can only be thankful he didn't stay in Nazareth.

We can only be thankful ministry pioneers in our day don't give up and quit.

We can only be thankful that many people in this congregation today, perhaps also you, have decided to bloom where they're planted, and to become instruments of God. That's hopeful for our shared future.

God always prospers the work of the faithful, even in ways we don't anticipate.

Rejoice and be glad!

Epiphany 3
Mark 1:14-20

## We Need Some Good News

*Now after John was arrested, Jesus came to Galilee, proclaiming the good news of God, and saying, "The time is fulfilled, and the kingdom of God has come near; repent, and believe in the good news." As Jesus passed along the Sea of Galilee, he saw Simon and his brother Andrew casting a net into the sea—for they were fishermen. And Jesus said to them, "Follow me and I will make you fish for people." And immediately they left their nets and followed him. As he went a little farther, he saw James son of Zebedee and his brother John, who were in their boat mending the nets. Immediately he called them; and they left their father Zebedee in the boat with the hired men, and followed him.*
Mark 1:14-20

Author Bruce Bawer, a layman within the Episcopal Church, has written a book with a provocative title. *Stealing Jesus* is a cautionary tale. It argues, convincingly, that within the past fifty years or so the clear intent of the Christian message has been taken hostage and perverted by elements within the American church community, groups determined to redefine what it means to be Christian.

Bawer's main argument is that when a movement takes a classic tradition and reinvents it for its own purposes, dangerous things happen. In this case, says Bawer, extreme fundamentalist religiosity has turned good news into bad news. To put it into theological terms, the gospel — God's healing, freeing, forgiving, life-giving love — is replaced with Law — a regimen requiring church folk to obey a set of religious requirements, or else risk damnation.

An example Bawer cites, and which many thoughtful Christian teachers have been echoing for decades, is the way the word evangelical has been revised and edited, so that the term has been emptied of its original rich meaning.

"Evangelical" is based on a Greek word. In Greek, *eu* means "good"; *angelion* means "message." The Greek word *euangelion*, which appears often in the New Testament and on which the English word evangelical is based, means, literally, "good news."

Perhaps by accident, but more likely by design and intent on the part of individuals within the most conservative wing of American Christianity, the term "evangelical" has come to mean, in both the public media and (as a result) in popular imagination, the name of an entire movement of "Bible believing Christians."

There are at least two problems with this 'hostage taking' of an excellent New Testament word. In the first place, it suggests that only certain kinds of Christians are truly evangelical. In the second place, it overlooks the fact that Christians of this sort are more often than not the opposite of real "evangelical" believers.

A more accurate understanding of "evangelical" would be the treatment it received at the beginning of the Protestant Reformation in Germany. The movement enabled by Martin Luther and his principled stand against the leadership of his own church came to be known as "evangelical." And it was that, in the truest sense of the word.

Martin Luther understood that the good news of the New Testament was nothing less than radical grace. God embraces a troubled, broken, desperate world with unconditional love. It cannot be earned nor merited. It comes as pure gift.

That is the good news Jesus came proclaiming. In the gospel reading for today, Jesus' message is very briefly stated: "[He] came to Galilee, proclaiming the good news of God, and saying, 'The time is fulfilled, and the kingdom of God has come near; repent and believe in the good news.' "

To this day, a visitor to Germany will discover two versions of Christianity, 'Evangelische' and 'Katholische.' These are the names attached, respectively, to the Lutheran and Roman Catholic expressions of the Christian Church in Germany. German Protestants who visit in the United States are understandably confused — perhaps even baffled — by the unconventional and peculiar use to which the term 'evangelical' has been put on this side of the Atlantic Ocean.

The most unfortunate (and, truthfully, perverse) aspect of how 'evangelical' is used in the American media is this: a word that originally meant "good news" now, more often than not, has come to mean "bad news." Evangelical churches frequently claim they preach "good news" but then proceed to proclaim "bad news" — law and warning instead of radical, unconditional free grace.

When he came preaching, Jesus did not put limits on God's good news. He did offer a warning, but it was not one that suggested "good behavior" was a precondition for God's grace. The warning was that a person can turn his or her back on God and miss the promised gift.

That's the meaning of Jesus' invitation, "Repent and believe in the gospel." To repent means to stop on the road you've been traveling, turn completely around, and head in the opposite direction. The implication is clear. Anyone needing repentance is heading on a path away from God, not toward a full life of love, grace, and mercy. That's why repentance so important. Good news comes without price, without condition; but a person can miss it by turning away from it.

Jesus may have been the original "evangelical." He came proclaiming the best news possible. God is for us. God is not hiding somewhere. God is not far away. God is not a cruel taskmaster. God is as near to us as the ground we walk on, as the blood that flows through our veins and as the breath that fills our lungs.

The first Christians came to understand God as their Hebrew ancestors did: God is life — and everything that has life is from and in God. That would be bad news if God were an angry judge (as Martin Luther first believed). But since God is the source of all good, the One in whom we live and move and have our being, knowing that this Good One is near, as Jesus came proclaiming, is good news indeed.

Everyone needs good news. Jesus says it's here. It's near and in our midst, as immediate as our breathing and our heartbeat.

Rejoice and be glad!

Epiphany 4
Mark 1:21-28

# Where's the Authenticity?

*They went to Capernaum; and when the sabbath came, he entered the synagogue and taught. They were astounded at his teaching, for he taught them as one having authority, and not as the scribes. Just then there was in their synagogue a man with an unclean spirit, and he cried out, "What have you to do with us, Jesus of Nazareth? Have you come to destroy us? I know who you are, the Holy One of God." But Jesus rebuked him, saying, "Be silent, and come out of him!" And the unclean spirit, convulsing him and crying with a loud voice, came out of him. They were all amazed, and they kept on asking one another, "What is this? A new teaching—with authority! He commands even the unclean spirits, and they obey him." At once his fame began to spread throughout the surrounding region of Galilee.*
Mark 1:21-28

Words are cheap. They can also be deadly if used improperly. One of our tasks and opportunities as human beings, endowed with brains capable of critical thinking, is to learn to discern what is to be believed and trusted and what is not.

During the run-up to a recent presidential election, a cartoon appeared in a national magazine. It showed a flock of sheep grazing on a hillside. In view of the flock was a large billboard showing a wolf wearing a business suit, smiling and flashing sharp, white teeth. The message below the picture of the wolf read, "I am going to eat you!"

Since it was a cartoon, the sheep could talk (as could the wolf pictured on the signboard). Obviously impressed with what he was reading, one sheep said to another, while glancing toward the billboard, "He says what he thinks. You have to be impressed with how convincing he sounds."

Indeed.

A significant part of Jesus' work among the simple folk in rural Galilee involved using words. He got a reputation, almost from the beginning, according to Mark, the earliest gospel writer, for being really good at it. A recurring theme among Jesus' listeners was, "He speaks with authority." They were obviously impressed.

In the text for today, a contrast is set before the reader and listener. Jesus knows how to use words. So do the scribes, representatives of the religious establishment in Palestine during the first century. Both Jesus and the scribes were good with words. The question was, who was to be believed?

Talk is cheap. Even when the speaker is a golden-throated orator with a silver tongue, the message can ring hollow. Deception easily results if one doesn't learn to discern its reliability.

Why did the common folk in Galilee no longer trust the scribes? There were plenty of reasons for them to have wanted to. These religiously trained leaders knew a lot. They could explain in great detail the meaning of the tradition into which the Galileean peasants had been born, and which they had grown up embracing. They were the religious experts. If you challenged one of them in a debate, they would most likely defeat and humiliate you. That's how well-versed they were.

But the scribes didn't speak with authority. There was nothing compelling or persuasive in their message. And there was nothing to authenticate it.

Why was Jesus different? We are told in today's reading from Mark's first chapter that Jesus spoke well — persuasively, impressively, passionately, in fact. But he married his words with actions that authenticated what he said.

The phrase, "He speaks with authority," appears twice in the reading. The first time, it comes after the teaching Jesus shares. The second time, it comes after he has brought healing to a man terrorized by an evil spirit.

Authentic words, authentic action. Convincing, persuasive messaging. It was all there. "He speaks with authority."

It has been wisely cautioned, "Don't believe everything you hear." It has become something of a standing joke to hear or say, "It must be true. I read it in the newspapers." Today that foolish "wisdom" has been expanded to include what we can read and hear on the internet, on unfiltered television "news" and over-the-top opinion channels, and even in the marketplace, where talk is cheap.

What gives authority to the flood of verbiage to which we are now subjected? Simply put, it is the authentic activity that matches the talk. When those two things intersect, the messenger gains credibility and we properly accord him or her the accolade, "This one speaks with authority."

Jesus' followers, including all of us, face an interesting challenge. If we are to be reliable conduits of the words shared by the messenger — the one who spoke 'with authority' — we will need to learn to marry our sincere words with authentic action. Jesus made it clear what is at the heart of Christianity: embraced by a loving God, we are to love as Jesus did — God, ourselves, and others.

This is not an easy assignment. But it can be done. Jesus did it first. We have his pattern to imitate. Thankfully, many in this congregation are doing it right now.

Talk is cheap — until we enrich it with our service. When we do that, we authenticate the message that was first given us. Like our Lord, empowered by his abiding presence, we, too, can — and do and will — speak with authority. As often as that happens, transformation happens in our world. And we can be a part of it.

Rejoice and be glad!

Epiphany 5
Mark 1:29-39

# Be Healed!

*As soon as they left the synagogue, they entered the house of Simon and Andrew, with James and John. Now Simon's mother-in-law was in bed with a fever, and they told him about her at once. He came and took her by the hand and lifted her up. Then the fever left her, and she began to serve them. That evening, at sundown, they brought to him all who were sick or possessed with demons. And the whole city was gathered around the door. And he cured many who were sick with various diseases, and cast out many demons; and he would not permit the demons to speak, because they knew him. In the morning, while it was still very dark, he got up and went out to a deserted place, and there he prayed. And Simon and his companions hunted for him. When they found him, they said to him, "Everyone is searching for you." He answered, "Let us go on to the neighboring towns, so that I may proclaim the message there also; for that is what I came out to do." And he went throughout Galilee, proclaiming the message in their synagogues and casting out demons.*
Mark 1:29-39

    A lot of damage has been done to the idea of wellness by "faith healers." They are not as prevalent in present day American culture as they once were. Decades ago, people with ailments of all sorts would flock to the services of radio / television preacher Oral Roberts. He had the reputation of laying his hands on the diseased parts of the bodies of his supplicants and praying over them. Frequently he would conclude his ritual by commanding the person, "Be healed!"
    Some of the sick pilgrims claimed they were made well. Many admitted afterwards that nothing really changed. On

rare occasion someone would reveal that they were complicit in a scheme to make a dramatic healing appear to have happened when, in fact, no such thing really had.

The activity of faith healers raises a legitimate question. Do healings actually happen, apart from medical treatment? If they do, what is really at work at such times?

Today's gospel reading details the very beginning of Jesus' active ministry according to the earliest of all the New Testament gospels. Mark tells of two such occurrences. A woman with a fever, confined to her bed, was healed. Later, perhaps in the same house, a great crowd gathered and more healings took place.

In the first instance, the healing was administered to Simon Peter's mother-in-law. The report of this event, which appears only in Mark, has proven awkward for those who believe that clergy should not marry. Clearly Peter, who is believed by some to have become the first pope in Rome, was married — and had a mother-in-law.

The second incident includes people with all sorts of ailments. Jesus guaranteed his growing fame and celebrity by offering healing to those needing it within a large crowd of seekers.

It is a fair question to ask: When Jesus healed people, what exactly was going on?

There is no good evidence to suggest that the writer of Mark believed Jesus was divine. At the outset he calls Jesus 'The Son of God,' but he does not explain what he thinks this means, and may have thought Jesus was adopted by God for special service, as the kings of Israel seem to have believed they had been when they were enthroned.

Mark may have believed that Jesus received divine power at his baptism, but even that is only speculation. When the voice from heaven announces he is "God's Son," it is with language that appears in the Old Testament Psalms, always used for royalty on coronation day.

How, then, was Jesus able to heal people?

Theologian and scholar John Dominic Crossan offers an interesting possible explanation. In the first place, Jesus was not the only person in Palestine, or even elsewhere in the Roman Empire, who was going about healing people. It is not commonly known today who these people were, but first century scholars have identified several by name.

More to the point, however, Crossan makes a distinction between 'curing' and 'healing.' He believes that Jesus did none of the former but a lot of the latter. Here is his argument:

If someone was dying of stage four cancer, Jesus would not have been able to reverse the process (even though nobody in the Roman empire knew what cancer was). In other words, Jesus did not cure diseases as modern medicine does.

But Jesus was a healer. He addressed what some have called "soul sickness." There are spiritual and psychological conditions which, if not addressed, can keep people from getting well. Once the underlying dis-ease (anxiety, lack of emotional well-being, feelings of distress) has been addressed, the patient can recover. It may well be that this was Jesus' contribution to the health and wellness of the many people he healed.

The question naturally arises: If Jesus was God's special person but not necessarily divine, according to Mark, and if he had about himself the ability to enable healing from soul-sickness, should his followers not also be able to do this? The answer is, Yes!

When sending them out on ministry assignment, Jesus is reported to have commanded his followers to heal people. In the Book of Acts there are stories of healings by leaders of the faith community, following Jesus' crucifixion.

In our own day, there are many ways that holistic medicine tries to incorporate 'healing and wellness' practices, in combination with medical treatment, in order to enable cures of the sick.

In some congregations there now exists a program called 'Stephen Ministries.' It incorporates best practices of parish nursing and helps individuals in the local congregation learn how to bring healing to those in need of it. None of these local volunteers are equipped to cure diseases, but all of them learn the fine art of healing care. There are countless stories of wellness resulting from their visits.

There is another aspect of healing not mentioned in this text. There is an ongoing need — and possibility — for the healing of relationships. Any caring Christian can be a part of such a ministry. Pastors enable it through counseling (and members who are hurting should not hesitate to contact their local clergy for help). But lay folk can also be instruments of healing. Broken relationships abound. Individuals who know how to listen, speak wisely — and sometimes lay hands upon those in stressed relationships — can help make whole what is fractured.

Be healed! Oral Roberts regularly used that command when he sensationalized his own ability to heal. It doesn't take a faith healer for wellness and wholeness to result. It takes those whom God has already made whole, and who are ready to make it happen. It is happening in our midst, right now.

Rejoice and be glad!

Transfiguration Sunday
Mark 9:2-9

# He's Not Who We Thought

*Six days later, Jesus took with him Peter and James and John, and led them up a high mountain apart, by themselves. And he was transfigured before them, and his clothes became dazzling white, such as no one on earth could bleach them. And there appeared to them Elijah with Moses, who were talking with Jesus. Then Peter said to Jesus, "Rabbi, it is good for us to be here; let us make three dwellings, one for you, one for Moses, and one for Elijah." He did not know what to say, for they were terrified. Then a cloud overshadowed them, and from the cloud there came a voice, "This is my Son, the Beloved; listen to him!" Suddenly when they looked around, they saw no one with them anymore, but only Jesus. As they were coming down the mountain, he ordered them to tell no one about what they had seen, until after the Son of Man had risen from the dead.*
Mark 9:2-9

There is something strange, almost jarring, about the appearance, exactly in the middle of the sixteenth chapter gospel of Mark, of a story about an other-worldly sound-and-light show on top of a mountain. The report of what we have come to call "The Transfiguration of Our Lord" doesn't seem to fit where it appears in Mark's gospel.

Think about it. Before he gives us the story of Jesus with two Old Testament prophets, being glorified in a blaze of light, Mark reports that Jesus' disciples were, to put it mildly, uncomprehending, dull-witted dolts who couldn't figure anything out. They were not especially convinced that Jesus was the real deal. One would think that, after going up the mountain with Jesus, at least three of his disciples would have had their lives and their attitudes about Jesus completely transformed. But that does not appear to have happened.

So, did it really happen?

This story appears in Matthew and Mark as well. But in all of those versions of the gospel story, Peter, who is described as having been present at the Transfiguration, does not seem to be a paragon of loyalty and virtue when the tough times came during the last week of Jesus' life. Why not?

The best answer we can give is that The Transfiguration has been artificially shoe-horned into the middle of Mark's gospel by the writer himself — and Matthew and Luke decided to follow suit.

Why did Mark do it?

Here's the most convincing answer Bible scholars can offer. Mark, who wrote the earliest gospel, set the pattern for the other three New Testament stories about Jesus. But his gospel ends frustratingly. His story of Jesus' resurrection, which ends at verse eight, seems woefully inadequate. (Everything after verse eight in his final chapter is material added by later writers.)

According to the ending of Mark's gospel, the resurrection of Jesus was extremely low-key. Only women went to the empty tomb. There was a young man there but no angel. The women ran away in terror, not telling anyone else anything.

Understandably, the other three gospel writers didn't like Mark's ending. They all tell the resurrection story in much greater, and far more glorious, detail. And the serious reader of the New Testament is left to ask: What happened to Mark? Why didn't he give us a better Resurrection story?

Again, the scholars have a suggestion, one that makes good sense. Mark actually does have a resurrection story. It's in chapter nine. It's the Transfiguration account. Does that make sense? Yes, when you think about it. Even though it interrupts Mark's narrative and seems jarring to those of us who like a logical progression in the stories we hear and read, the gospel writer seems to have decided that we need 'a little bit of Easter' on the way to Holy Week. Why? Because, without that, readers will get the wrong idea about Jesus. (Especially because, for his own reasons, Mark wants his Easter morning story to be bare-bones spare.)

The Jesus who is going to Jerusalem to speak truth to power, and who ends up dying when his followers thought he should have won the day — this Jesus isn't who they thought he was. He isn't who we think he is.

Mark started his gospel story, in the very first verse of chapter one, announcing that Jesus was 'the Son of God.' He doesn't explain what he means by that. According to Mark, Jesus may not have been infused with divine energy before his baptism. We're not sure what Mark really thinks happened at the Jordan River. But clearly Jesus was God's special agent, the one who came among us to make clear what God means for our lives.

The disciples saw Jesus as a very wise teacher, one who 'spoke with authority' and could wow the crowds. But an agent of God's love for the entire world and transformation of all humankind? Maybe, maybe not.

Into the middle of this strange ministry of Jesus, Mark places what amounts to a preview of Easter. We should not read the Transfiguration story as literal history. It is a foreshadowing of the risen Christ. He's not who we think he is. He's a good deal more than that.

This story is Mark's way of saying to us, as we read about the horror to come — Jesus' victimization at the hands of his enemies — that you can't kill the truth by killing the messenger. You can't get rid of love by opposing it with hate. You can't stop the future from breaking in by holding tightly to a dying past.

Jesus is not going to Jerusalem to become a loser for a lost cause. He's not what he probably looked like to the disciples, when the landscape began to turn dark and grim for their movement. Jesus is the shape of the future. The powerful love for all of us which he demonstrated, standing up to and facing down his killers, was not meaningless and empty.

We won't be getting rid of Jesus. He's going to be around, in our midst, filling our future.

That's what the Transfiguration story means for us. And the Jesus we see there can't be dismissed — because this Jesus, who isn't who we thought he was, isn't going away.

Rejoice and be glad!

www.ingramcontent.com/pod-product-compliance
Lightning Source LLC
Chambersburg PA
CBHW072015060426
42446CB00043B/2556